The Cybersecurity Maturity Model Certification (CMMC)

A pocket guide

The Cybersecurity Maturity Model Certification (CMMC)

A pocket guide

WILLIAM GAMBLE

IT Governance Publishing

Every possible effort has been made to ensure that the information contained in this book is accurate at the time of going to press, and the publisher and the author cannot accept responsibility for any errors or omissions, however caused. Any opinions expressed in this book are those of the author, not the publisher. Websites identified are for reference only, not endorsement, and any website visits are at the reader's own risk. No responsibility for loss or damage occasioned to any person acting, or refraining from action, as a result of the material in this publication can be accepted by the publisher or the author.

IT Governance Publishing Ltd
Unit 3, Clive Court
Bartholomew's Walk
Cambridgeshire Business Park
Ely, Cambridgeshire
CB7 4EA
United Kingdom
www.itgovernancepublishing.co.uk

First published in the United Kingdom in 2020 by IT Governance Publishing.

ISBN 978-1-78778-244-0

ABOUT THE AUTHOR

William Gamble is an international cybersecurity and privacy compliance expert. He is one of the few lawyers to hold advanced cybersecurity professional qualifications, and has an in-depth understanding of the design, management, and deployment of technology within the ISO 27001 framework.

With more than 30 years' experience of international regulatory practice in the U.S., EU, China, and other countries, William has had hundreds of articles published globally, written three books, and appeared on numerous radio and television programs around the world.

William is a member of the Florida Bar and several federal courts. His qualifications include Juris Doctor (JD), Master of Laws (LLM), CompTIA® A+, Network+, Security+, CASP (Advanced Security Practitioner), ISO 27001 Lead Auditor and Lead Implementer, and GDPR Practitioner (GDPR P).

CONTENTS

CHAPTER 1: AN INTRODUCTION TO THE US DEPARTMENT OF DEFENSE DIGITAL SUPPLY CHAIN

The US Department of Defense (DoD) is one of the largest employers in the world. It employs about 2.87 million people,[1] and has a base budget of $671 billion, and a $69 billion budget for overseas contingency operations for the 2021 fiscal year.[2] It also engages about 350,000 contractors.

These contractors represent the Department's supply chain. They also present a security risk – a problem familiar to many businesses. Supply chains need to be managed to be efficient, economical and effective. One objective is to avoid single points of failure, because like a regular chain, a supply chain is only as strong as its weakest link.

This concept has not gone unnoticed by cyber thieves. For any information to have value, it must be shared. Information is shared widely across digital supply chains, offering criminals a major opportunity to steal it.

Cyber thieves, whether they are large criminal organizations or foreign adversarial governments, try to be efficient. Attacking a large, well-defended organization can be a frustrating and costly endeavor. Rather than targeting the organization directly, they have found that it is far easier and cheaper to go after contractors and partners, which are often less secure and can be used to gain a foothold in the main target's networks.

This method has been used very successfully against a number of large corporations and has been responsible for many of the largest cybersecurity breaches. Take the example of Target. In 2013, the US retailer lost the credit and debit card information

---

[1] www.defense.gov/our-story/.

[2] www.americanprogress.org/issues/security/reports/2020/05/06/48462 0/pentagons-fiscal-year-2021-budget-meets-u-s-national-security-needs/.

of more than 40 million shoppers who had visited the store during the holiday season. The total cost of the data breach, according to Target, was $202 million.[3]

The criminals did not directly attack Target, instead targeting a vendor to gain access. A simple Google search of Target's supplier portal provided the hackers with a wealth of information about vendors and suppliers, including how to interact with the company, submit invoices, etc. They used this list to surveil contractors and, using a simple phishing email, managed to trick an employee of refrigeration contractor Fazio Mechanical into downloading malware. Once installed, it was simply a matter of time before the criminals were able to gain access to Target's customer database.

Target is not alone; "The average enterprise connects to 1,586 partners via the cloud",[4] but often vastly underestimates the risk from these partners, which can include vendors, suppliers, agencies, consultants, and any company with which it does business. While larger enterprises tend to have extensive security infrastructure, smaller companies in the supply chain often have fewer measures in place, leaving them open to breaches. This allows the criminal to gain a foothold in a partner's network, and from there infiltrate bigger targets.

The problem with the DoD is infinitely larger. It connects with partners all over the world, each of which represents a major security risk for the keeper of the US's most precious secrets.

To address the issue, in 2015 the DoD wrote a regulation: 48 CFR § 252.204-7012 – Safeguarding Covered Defense Information and Cyber Incident Reporting. Its purpose was to codify contractors' cybersecurity responsibilities and procedures by altering the contractual requirements

---

[3] *www.thesslstore.com/blog/2013-target-data-breach-settled/*.

[4] *www.darkreading.com/perimeter/beware-the-hidden-risk-of-business-partners-in-the-cloud/a/d-id/1321841*.

implemented through the Federal Acquisition Regulation (FAR) and Defense FAR Supplement (DFARS).

The regulation, generally referred to as DFARS 252.204-7012 or DFARS 7012, requires all DoD contractors to "provide adequate security on all covered contractor information systems."[5] It defines 'adequate security' as "protective measures that are commensurate with the consequences and probability of loss, misuse, or unauthorized access to, or modification of information."[6] Furthermore, covered contractor information systems that are not part of an IT service or system operated on behalf of the US government "shall be subject to the security requirements in National Institute of Standards and Technology (NIST) Special Publication (SP) 800-171, "Protecting Controlled Unclassified Information in Nonfederal Information Systems and Organizations".[7]

NIST SP 800-171 is a codification of the requirements that any non-federal computer system must follow in order to store, process, or transmit Controlled Unclassified Information (CUI) or provide security protection for such systems. This document is based on the Federal Information Security Management Act of 2002 (FISMA) Moderate-level requirements. The first version was promulgated in 2015. Revision 2 came out in February 2020.

NIST SP 800-171 is a list of controls taken from NIST SP 800-53 Rev. 4. It includes 110 controls in 14 security families. It is generally considered a condensed version of NIST SP 800-53, which is a catalog of security and privacy controls for federal information systems and organizations to protect organizational operations, organizational assets, individuals, other organizations, and the nation from a diverse set of threats,

---

[5] *www.law.cornell.edu/cfr/text/48/252.204-7012*.

[6] Ibid.

[7] Ibid.

including hostile cyber attacks, natural disasters, structural failures, and human errors. In short, everything.

In contrast NIST SP 800-171 is more focused. It is meant to protect the confidentiality of CUI if the CUI is resident in non-federal (private) information systems organizations. CUI includes numerous categories. It may not be considered classified, but it is still exceptionally important and can be very sensitive. CUI categories include:

- Critical infrastructure
- Government financial information
- Immigration information
- Intelligence information
- Law enforcement information
- Criminal records
- Nuclear information
- Patent applications
- Health information
- Taxpayer information, and many others[8]

DFARS 252.204-7012 required contractors to implement NIST SP 800-171 as soon as practical, but they had to demonstrate implementation by December 31, 2017. However, despite potential penalties such as contract revocation, this requirement was largely ignored and many contractors did not adopt NIST SP 800-171.

The DoD tried to incentivize them, with contractors that adopted NIST SP 800-171 considered to have a competitive advantage within the contract awards process. Nevertheless, many chose to put off compliance. Worse, there are even reported cases of DoD

---

[8] For more information, see: *www.archives.gov/cui/registry/category-list*.

contractors falsely stating that they were NIST SP 800-171 compliant on DoD contracts.

The Cybersecurity Maturity Model Certification (CMMC)

Published in January 2020, the CMMC verifies that contractors have adopted the NIST SP 800-171 framework and are meeting essential cybersecurity requirements before the contract is awarded. The CMMC is not a self-certification program; instead, all companies conducting business with the DoD, including subcontractors, must be certified by an independent third-party commercial certification organization.

To create the CMMC program, the DoD (specifically the Office of the Under Secretary of Defense for Acquisition and Sustainment (OUSD(A&S)) partnered with Carnegie Mellon University Software Engineering Institute (SEI), John Hopkins University Applied Physics Laboratory (APL) and the CMMC Center of Excellence (CMMC-COE)/IT Acquisition Advisory Council (IT-AAC).

The CMMC program relies on several other cybersecurity models such as the NIST Cybersecurity Framework, ISO 27001 and the Payment Card Industry Data Security Standard (PCI DSS). Government agencies are already subject to the Federal Information Security Management Act (FISMA), which outlines mandatory guidelines to strengthen the security of government information systems. The Act requires each federal agency to develop, document, and implement an agency-wide program to secure the information and information systems that support the agency's operations and assets.

FISMA is a certification and accreditation process. It is the source of the annual Federal Computer Security Report Card, which is a measure used to determine how well US agencies perform. The process is similar to the Federal Risk and Authorization Management Program (FedRAMP) in that both were developed as a framework for assessing agency security to give Authority to Operate (ATO), and both depend on the NIST guidelines. The frameworks have four similar phases:

1. **Initiation:** Includes preparation, resource identification, and system analysis, including initial risk assessment, independent audit, and system testing. In the FedRAMP process this phase is called 'Initiating', and also involves applying for the assessment.
2. **Security Certification:** Includes security control assessment and certification documentation. Under FISMA, entities must verify that system controls are properly implemented as outlined in the initiation phase. In contrast, under FedRAMP the assessment has to be made by an independent third-party assessment organization (3PAO).
3. **Security Accreditation:** Includes accreditation decision and documentation. During this phase, entities must examine if the remaining risk, after implementing security controls in the previous phase, is acceptable. Under FISMA, the accreditation decision is made by an authorizing official (AO) who is a senior (federal) official or executive with the authority to formally assume responsibility for operating an information system at an acceptable level of risk to organizational operations. In FedRAMP, this decision is made by the FedRAMP Joint Authorization Board (JAB) or another certified agency.
4. **Continuous Monitoring:** Includes system configuration, security management, monitoring, and reporting. This phase focuses on maintaining a high level of security by monitoring security controls, documenting any updates, and determining if any new vulnerabilities develop.

FedRAMP is reserved only for agencies or Cloud service providers that currently use or plan to use a Cloud solution to host federal information. It is a "do once, use many times" framework for the assessment of Cloud products and services and, as such, is a far more stringent authorization process.

Anyone familiar with ISO 27001, the international standard for information security management, will immediately see similarities between the four phases and W. Edward Deming's Plan-Do-Check-Act (PDCA) cycle upon which the ISO framework is based. The four phases in this case can be viewed as Plan (initiation), Do (implementation), Check (accreditation), Act (monitor and improve). The CMMC also incorporates other aspects of the ISO process, specifically audits by an independent third party.

CHAPTER 2: TERMS AND DEFINITIONS

The following highlighted terms and definitions are cited from resources provided in the footnotes. Not all of them are discussed in this pocket guide, but you may come across any or all of these terms when dealing with the DoD, therefore this chapter serves as a guide to navigate some of the most common acronyms you may encounter on your CMMC implementation journey.

The CMMC Accreditation Body (CMMC-AB)

The CMMC Accreditation Body is authorized by the US Department of Defense to be the sole authoritative source for the operationalization of CMMC Assessments and Training with the DOD contractor community, or other communities that may adopt the CMMC.[9]

The CMMC Body of Knowledge (CMMC-BOK)

The CMMC-BOK will be a centralized source of information that will specify training objectives for assessor certification levels in order to ensure quality and standardization.

---

[9] *www.cmmcab.org/*.

The CMMC-Center of Excellence (CMMC-COE)

An IT-AAC sponsored and hosted public – private partnership that will be the focal point for coordination, communication, and collaboration in support of entities seeking to achieve the Cybersecurity Maturity Model Certification requirements, to improve and enhance the cybersecurity and overall security of the supply chain for the defense industrial base and the United States Department of Defense.[10]

Controlled Technical Information (CTI)

Controlled Technical Information means technical information with military or space application that is subject to controls on the access, use, reproduction, modification, performance, display, release, disclosure, or dissemination.[11]

Controlled Unclassified Information (CUI)

Information that requires safeguarding or dissemination controls pursuant to and consistent with law, regulations, and government-wide policies, excluding information that is classified under Executive Order 13526.[12]

Covered Defense Information (CDI)

Term used to identify information that requires protection under DFARS Clause 252.204-7012.[13]

---

[10] *https://cmmc-coe.org/about-us/*.

[11] *www.archives.gov/cui/registry/category-detail/controlled-technical-info.html*.

[12] *www.acq.osd.mil/cmmc/docs/CMMC_Appendices_V1.02_20200318.pdf*.

[13] Ibid.

Critical Infrastructure, sometimes referred to as Essential Critical Infrastructure

Critical infrastructure describes the physical and cyber systems and assets that are so vital to the United States that their incapacity or destruction would have a debilitating impact on our physical or economic security or public health or safety.[14]

Defense Industrial Base (DIB)

The worldwide industrial complex that enables research and development, as well as design, production, delivery, and maintenance of military weapons systems, subsystems, and components or parts, to meet U.S. military requirements.[15]

Defense Industrial Base Cybersecurity Program (DIBNet)

DoD established the Defense Industrial Base (DIB) Cybersecurity (CS) Program to enhance and supplement DIB participants' capabilities to safeguard DoD information that resides on or transits DIB unclassified networks or information systems. This public-private cybersecurity partnership is designed to improve DIB network defenses, reduce damage to critical programs, and increase DoD and DIB cyber situational awareness.[16]

DoD Cyber Crime Center (DC3)

DC3's mission is to deliver superior digital and multimedia (D/MM) forensic services, cyber technical training, vulnerability sharing, technical solutions development, and cyber analysis within the following DoD mission areas: cybersecurity and critical infrastructure protection, law

---

[14] *www.dhs.gov/topic/critical-infrastructure-security*.

[15] *www.acq.osd.mil/cmmc/docs/CMMC_Appendices_V1.02_20200318. pdf*.

[16] *https://dibnet.dod.mil/portal/intranet/*.

enforcement and counterintelligence, document and media exploitation, and counterterrorism.[17]

Enterprise Mission Assurance Support Service (eMASS)

eMASS is a government owned web-based application with a broad range of services for comprehensive fully integrated cybersecurity management. Features include dashboard reporting, controls scorecard measurement, and the generation of a system security authorization package.[18]

Federal Risk and Authorization Management Program (FedRAMP)

The Federal Risk and Authorization Management Program (FedRAMP) is a government-wide program that provides a standardized approach to security assessment, authorization, and continuous monitoring for cloud products and services.[19]

Medium Assurance Certificate

In order to report cyber incidents [...] the contractor or subcontractor shall have or acquire a DoD-approved medium assurance certificate to report cyber incidents.[20]

For information about how to attain a medium assurance certificate, see: *http://public.cyber.mil/eca*.

---

[17] *www.dc3.mil/*.

[18] *www.dcsa.mil/is/emass/*.

[19] *www.fedramp.gov/about/*.

[20] *www.law.cornell.edu/cfr/text/32/236.4*.

Plan of Action and Milestones (POA&M)

POA&M Management assists Information System Security Officer (ISSO) with reviewing, monitoring, and facilitating closure of weaknesses identified during Security Assessment and Authorization (SA&A) process.[21]

System Security Plan (SSP)

A system security plan (SSP) is a document that outlines how an organization implements its security requirements. An SSP outlines the roles and responsibilities of security personnel. It details the different security standards and guidelines that the organization follows.[22]

---

[21] "Security Consultation Services (SCS) Plan of Action and Milestones (POA&M)", *www.cisa.gov/risk-management-strategy.*

[22]*www.acq.osd.mil/cmmc/docs/CMMC_Appendices_V1.02_20200318. pdf.*

CHAPTER 3: WHO NEEDS TO COMPLY WITH THE CMMC?

The CMMC was developed for all government contractors (herein after Organizations Seeking Certification or OSCs) that process federal contract information (FCI) and CUI. It applies to both primary contractors and subcontractors, who will have until the US 2026 fiscal year to demonstrate CMMC compliance.

The first ten Requests for Information (RFIs) that include CMMC requirements were scheduled to appear at the end of July/early August 2020. The Requests for Proposals (RFPs) will follow in early 2021 and the first contract awards are expected to follow shortly after.[23] The program will eventually expand to all DoD procurement and it is expected that CMMC requirements will be in all new RFIs by 2026. Existing contracts will not be modified to require the CMMC, with exceptions. However, as DoD contracts generally have a five-year contract cycle (one base plus four option years), after 2026 almost all DoD contractors will be required to achieve certification.

Maturity levels

Under the CMMC, all OSCs are not created equal. Although all are organizations that wish to bid on a DoD contract, each contract has different requirements. The first step is to determine what the contract requires. For example, lower-level contracts will require fewer controls, fewer documents, fewer audits, and less qualified auditors.

---

[23] All US government contracts have to go through various steps. The first step is for the government agency or department to issue a request for information (RFI), which is a preliminary document that vendors can complete to provide general information about the relevant products/services. Following this, the agency or department issues a request for proposal (RFP), which vendors can respond to with more detail and costs for a specific product/service.

Going forward, DoD contracts will state a specific CMMC level, based on the sensitivity of the information (FCI or CUI):

- **Level 1: "Basic Cyber Hygiene"** – This level requires the OSC to implement 17 controls from NIST SP 800-171. This level is only to safeguard FCI and is not for organizations processing CUI. It consists only of practices that correspond to basic safeguarding requirements specified in 48 CFR 52.204-2, considered the very basic or minimal number of controls to protect FCI.[24] Organizations may only be able to perform these controls in an ad hoc manner and may or may not rely on documentation.

- **Level 2: "Intermediate Cyber Hygiene"** – In order to pass an audit for this level, the OSC will need to implement another 48 controls from NIST SP 800-171 plus 7 new "Other" controls. An organization establishes and documents practices and policies to guide the implementation of the CMMC. The documentation of practices allows the organization to perform them in a repeatable manner. This is the lowest level at which organizations can process CUI. At this level, the controls must not only be performed, they also must be documented.

- **Level 3: "Good Cyber Hygiene"** – In order to pass an audit for this level, the OSC will need to implement the final 45 controls from NIST SP 800-171 Rev. 2 plus 14 new "Other" controls. An organization must establish,

---

[24] 48 CFR § 52.204-2 states that federal contracts with contractors have specific security requirements (Security Agreement (DD Form 441). These include general physical and legal security requirements and very basic cybersecurity. The implementation of these requirements is found in The National Industrial Security Program Operating Manual (DOD 5220.22-M).

maintain, and resource a plan demonstrating the management of activities for practice implementation. Level 3 focuses on the protection of CUI and encompasses all the security requirements specified in NIST SP 800-171 as well as additional practices noted in DFARS 252.204-7012.

- **Level 4: "Proactive"** – In order to pass an audit for this level, the OSC will need to implement an additional 13 controls from NIST SP 800-171 plus 13 new "Other" controls.
- **Level 5: "Advanced / Progressive"** – In order to pass an audit for this level, the OSC will need to implement the final 5 controls in NIST SP 800-172[25] plus 11 new "Other" controls.

Assessors

Any OSC considering bidding on a DoD contract should not only be familiar with the five levels of compliance, but also with the CMMC infrastructure. This is made up of four different types of people or organizations who can help the OSC with certification.

First are the consultants. There are two types of consultant:

1. Those who can help an organization prepare for audit
2. Those who actually conduct the audit to determine if the organization is compliant

---

[25] NIST SP 800-172 (formerly NIST 171B) is a supplement to NIST-171 and includes recommendations for enhanced security requirements to provide additional protection for Controlled Unclassified Information (CUI) in nonfederal systems and organizations, where such information is associated with critical programs or high value assets (HVA). It is specifically designed to respond to the advanced persistent threats (APT).

These consultants are categorized as Registered Practitioners (RPs), Certified Professionals (CPs), or Certified Assessors (CAs), depending on their level of training, knowledge, and experience. CAs are further subdivided into three categories: CA-1, CA-3, and CA-5.

These different designations are subject to different training requirements. The first level is RP. RPs deliver a non-certified advisory service informed by basic training on the CMMC. To become an RP requires registration, basic training, and CMMC-AB approval.

The next level is CP. To become a CP, the applicant must complete a CMMC-AB Certified Professional Class (CMMC model training) from a Licensed Training Provider (LTP), pass a commercial background check and participate in an assessment team.[26]

The next step is to become a CA, which allows the consultant to assess an organization. As stated earlier, the CMMC is not a self-certification process; instead, all companies conducting business with the DoD, including subcontractors, must be certified by an independent third party: the CAs. The designation of 1, 3, or 5 represents the highest-level organization a CA can assess. CA-1 can only assess the first level of OSC, CA-3 can assess up to level 3, and only CA-5 can assess all levels.

These categories also represent a career path of ever-increasing knowledge. The consultant starts out as an RP. They can become a CP by attending a CMMC-AB class and passing an exam. Once they are a CP, they can apply to become a CA-1. This requires the applicant to take another course and pass another exam, followed by an observed assessment.

A CA-1 can apply for CA-3 certification if they have at least four years of information technology experience. After that, they

---

[26] A background check must be completed by a CMMC-AB approved provider. These include – but are not limited to – checks of degrees, certifications, criminal records, employment history, motor vehicles, residence.

can apply to become a CA-5. This requires another exam, but the applicant must also have successfully completed 15 CA-5 assessments before they can get the training necessary to take the exam.

All CAs have to pass a background check. This can be a National Agency Check (NAC), Department of Homeland Security (DHS) Suitability credential, or other DoD-accepted clearance. CA-1 can be US persons, which includes permanent US residents who have a green card. CA-3 and above must be US citizens.

In addition to the CAs, there are Certified Instructors (CI) who will complete the training, Certified Master Instructors (CMIs), who will train the CIs, and certified Quality Auditors (QAs) who will review the CA's assessment and issue the certification to the OSC.

Organizations

All the individuals mentioned in the previous section usually work for one of three organizations:

1. The CMMC Accreditation Body (CMMC-AB)
2. A Certified Third-Party Assessment Organization (C3PAO)
3. An LTP

There are also Licensed Publishing Partners (LPPs), qualified publishers that are licensed by the CMMC-AB to create approved educational courses and content.

At the top of the food chain is the CMMC-AB, which is authorized by the DoD to establish, manage, control, and administer the CMMC assessment, certification, training, and accreditation processes for the DoD supply chain. It is a private nonprofit organization.

> The CMMC-AB establishes and oversees a qualified, trained, and high-fidelity community of assessors that can deliver consistent and informative assessments to

participating organizations against a defined set of controls/best practices within the Cybersecurity Maturity Model Certification (CMMC) Program.[27]

The CMMC-AB is a nod to the ISO accreditation bodies, which are usually national nonprofit organizations. The US ISO accreditation body is the ANSI National Accreditation Board (ANAB), which is a non-governmental organization that provides accreditation services and training to public- and private-sector organizations, serving the global marketplace. ANAB is the largest accreditation body in North America.

In the ISO world, accreditation bodies accredit certification bodies. It is the certification body that does the certification audit and issues the ISO certificate. In the CMMC world, the CA does the assessment, which is then checked by the QA, who works for the CMMC-AB. If the QA approves the assessment, the CMMC-AB issues the certificate.

Besides issuing the CMMC certificate, the CMMC-AB approves the training, exams, and any published material created by the LPPs.

Below the CMMC-AB are the C3PAOs. These are like the 3PAOs in the FedRAMP program, which review the security architecture of the Cloud applicant in accordance with FedRAMP requirements. Based on their review, they develop a Security Assessment Report (SAR) and complete assessment documentation. The assessment focuses on the applicant's specific functions, processes, procedures, and policies necessary to complete an assessment.

In the CMMC program, the C3PAOs fulfill a similar role. These organizations are contacted by OSCs through the CMMC Marketplace and schedule an assessment through the CMMC-

---

[27] *www.cmmcab.org/cmmc-standard*.

AB portal.[28] The C3PAO assesses according to the CMMC-AB Assessment Standard using the CMMC-AB Assessment Method using only the appropriate CA.

In many ways, the C3PAOs are comparable to certification bodies under the ISO framework, which can issue ISO certificates. To become a certification body, an organization has to get its own certificate from an accreditation body under the ISO 17021 procedure.[29] For now, C3PAOs are not required to get ISO 17021 certification, but that may change. Any requirements would be published on the CMMC-AB website: *www.cmmcab.org/c3pao-lp*.

However, C3PAOs do have other requirements. They have to have specific types of insurance. They have to sign a license agreement with the CMMC-AB. Like the CAs, they have to undergo a background check. They also have to have an association with at least one RP, CP, or CA.

Below the C3PAOs is another, more basic, organization – the Registered Provider Organization (RPO). Like an RP, these organizations can only help in CMMC preparation and offer non-certified consultative services. Their requirements are similar to a C3PAO. They must receive authorization from the CMMC-AB, sign an RPO agreement, and pass a background check. They also have to employ at least one RP.

---

[28] CMMC-AB is establishing a CMMC Marketplace that will include a list of approved C3PAOs, Certified Assessors (CA), Instructors, Certified Instructors (CI), Registered Practioners (RP), Registered Practioners Organizations (RPO), Licensed Training Providers (LTP) and Licensed Publishing Partners (LPP). For more information, see: *www.cmmcab.org/marketplace*.

[29] ISO/IEC 17021-1:2015 Conformity assessment: Requirements for bodies providing audit and certification of management systems is an international standard that contains principles and requirements for the competence, consistency and impartiality of bodies providing audit and certification of all types of management systems.

CHAPTER 4: CMMC IMPLEMENTATION

The whole point of the CMMC process goes back to the original requirement of DFARS 52.204-7012 – to provide 'adequate security'.

But what is adequate security? In the past the legislation would have created a set of controls as adequate security. This has changed. This test of adequate security is now known as the risk-based standard and is in line with most modern cybersecurity legislation around the world. It is similar to the EU's General Data Protection Regulation (GDPR) Article 32, which requires anyone who processes the information of EU residents to "implement appropriate technical and organisational measures to ensure a level of security appropriate to the risk."[30]

About 20 US states have similar requirements. One example is the California law §1798.81.5 (b), which requires that:

> A business that owns, licenses, or maintains personal information about a California resident shall implement and maintain reasonable security procedures and practices appropriate to the nature of the information."[31]

In this way, the CMMC process is part of a much larger global regulation that will require all businesses to adopt some sort of cybersecurity framework to protect the information they hold and process.

But which framework? For the most part, the CMMC model uses NIST SP 800-171 Rev. 2 (14 security families, 110 controls), which is based on Federal Information Processing Standards Publication 200 (FIPS 200), the standard that specifies the minimum security requirements for non-military federal

---

[30] *https://gdpr.eu/article-32-security-of-processing/*.

[31] *https://leginfo.legislature.ca.gov/faces/codes_displaySection.xhtml?lawCode=CIV&sectionNum=1798.81.5*.

information systems.[32] In fact, 48 CFR § 52.204-7012(b)(2)(i) states that "the covered contractor information system shall be subject to the security requirements in National Institute of Standards and Technology (NIST) Special Publication (SP) 800-171."

The NIST SP 800-171 has 14 security families. What NIST refers to as 'security families' are called 'domains' in the CMMC; with regard to this guide, these terms are functionally synonymous. For convenience, we will refer to them as 'domains' for the remainder of this pocket guide.

The 14 NIST SP 800-171 domains that make up the CMMC domains, are:

1. Access Control (AC)
2. Awareness and Training (AT)
3. Audit and Accountability (AU)
4. Configuration Management (CM)
5. Identification and Authentication (IA)
6. Incident Response (IR)
7. Maintenance (MA)
8. Media Protection (MP)
9. Personnel Security (PS)
10. Physical and Environmental Protection (PE)
11. Risk Assessment (RA)
12. Security Assessment (CA)
13. System and Communications Protection (SC)
14. System and Information Integrity (SI)

The DoD warns that the source for the CMMC controls is not limited to NIST SP 800-171:

> CMMC incorporates additional practices and processes from other standards, references, and/or sources such as NIST SP 800-53, Aerospace Industries Association (AIA)

---

[32] *https://csrc.nist.gov/publications/detail/fips/200/final*.

National Aerospace Standard (NAS) 9933 "Critical Security Controls for Effective Capability in Cyber Defense", and Computer Emergency Response Team (CERT) Resilience Management Model (RMM) v1.2.[33]

Thus, the CMMC has three more domains:

15. Asset Management (AM)
16. Situational Awareness (SA)
17. Recovery (RE)

With the additional practices, the total number of controls for levels 3,4 and 5 will be: level 3: 130; level 4: 156 and level 5: 171.

The areas represent a broad-based, balanced information security program that addresses the management, operational, and technical aspects of protecting federal information on non-federal information systems.

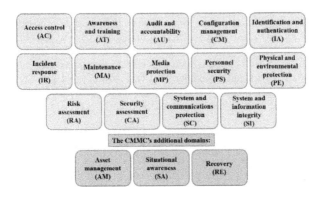

Figure 1: CMMC domains

---

[33] See section 8: "What is the relationship between the NIST SP 800-171 rev.1 and CMMC?", *www.acq.osd.mil/cmmc/faq.html*.

25

The 14 domains of NIST SP 800-171 Rev. 2

The CMMC contains all 14 domains in NIST SP 800-171. In this section, I provide a brief overview of each family, followed by the relevant extract from NIST SP 800-171 Rev. 2 covering the basic security requirements in more detail,[34] as well as including references to ISO 27001.

Each domain and the controls within that domain are as follows:

1: Access Control (AC)

Cyber security is about the preservation of confidentiality, integrity and availability. In order to achieve these goals organizations have to determine ways to limit information system access to authorized users and their devices. They also have to limit processes on these devices where they can. The best way to accomplish this is through the process known as access control.

Access control is one of the largest domains in NIST SP 800-171. It is also one of the largest domains in Annex A. In Annex A of ISO 27001, the access control category can be found in control set A.9. Most of the differences between NIST SP 800-171 and Annex A have to do with cataloging. Some controls in the Access Control section of NIST SP 800-171 (3.1.1–3.1.22) can be found in other areas of ISO 27001, either directly or in how the control is implemented (ISO 27002).

---

[34] The highlighted citations in this chapter are quoted from NIST SP 800-171 Rev. 2. For more information, see: *https://nvlpubs.nist.gov/nistpubs/SpecialPublications/NIST.SP.800-171r2.pdf*.

3.1 ACCESS CONTROL

Basic Security Requirements

3.1.1 Limit system access to authorized users, processes acting on behalf of authorized users, and devices (including other systems).

Access control policies (e.g., identity- or role-based policies, control matrices, and cryptography) control access between active entities or subjects (i.e., users or processes acting on behalf of users) and passive entities or objects (e.g., devices, files, records, and domains) in systems. Access enforcement mechanisms can be employed at the application and service level to provide increased information security. Other systems include systems internal and external to the organization. This requirement focuses on account management for systems and applications. The definition of and enforcement of access authorizations, other than those determined by account type (e.g., privileged verses non-privileged) are addressed in requirement 3.1.2.

3.1.2 Limit system access to the types of transactions and functions that authorized users are permitted to execute.

Organizations may choose to define access privileges or other attributes by account, by type of account, or a combination of both.

3.1.3 Control the flow of CUI in accordance with approved authorizations.

Information flow control regulates where information can travel within a system and between systems (versus who can access the information) and without explicit regard to subsequent accesses to that information.

3.1.4 Separate the duties of individuals to reduce the risk of malevolent activity without collusion.

Separation of duties addresses the potential for abuse of authorized privileges and helps to reduce the risk of malevolent activity without collusion.

3.1.5 Employ the principle of least privilege, including for specific security functions and privileged accounts.

Organizations employ the principle of least privilege for specific duties and authorized accesses for users and processes.

3.1.6 Use non-privileged accounts or roles when accessing nonsecurity functions.

This requirement limits exposure when operating from within privileged accounts or roles.

3.1.7 Prevent non-privileged users from executing privileged functions and capture the execution of such functions in audit logs.

Privileged functions include establishing system accounts, performing system integrity checks, conducting patching operations, or administering cryptographic key management activities.

3.1.8 Limit unsuccessful logon attempts.

Due to the potential for denial of service, automatic lockouts initiated by systems are, in most cases, temporary and automatically release after a predetermined period established by the organization (i.e., a delay algorithm).

3.1.9 Provide privacy and security notices consistent with applicable CUI rules.

System use notifications can be implemented using messages or warning banners displayed before individuals log in to organizational systems.

The design of these notices should take into account the relevant laws (e.g. GDPR, CCPA) applicable in the jurisdiction.

3.1.10 Use session lock with pattern-hiding displays to prevent access and viewing of data after a period of inactivity.

Session locks are temporary actions taken when users stop work and move away from the immediate vicinity of the system but do not want to log out because of the temporary nature of their absences.

3.1.11 Terminate (automatically) a user session after a defined condition.

This requirement addresses the termination of user-initiated logical sessions in contrast to the termination of network connections that are associated with communications sessions (i.e., disconnecting from the network).

3.1.12 Monitor and control remote access sessions.

Automated monitoring and control of remote access sessions allows organizations to detect cyber-attacks and help to ensure ongoing compliance with remote access policies by auditing connection activities of remote users on a variety of system components (e.g., servers, workstations, notebook computers, smart phones, and tablets).

3.1.13 Employ cryptographic mechanisms to protect the confidentiality of remote access sessions.

Cryptographic standards include FIPS-validated cryptography and NSA-approved cryptography.

Organizations often employ encrypted virtual private networks (VPNs) to enhance confidentiality over remote connections.

3.1.14 Route remote access via managed access control points.

Routing remote access through managed access control points enhances explicit, organizational control over such connections, reducing the susceptibility to unauthorized access to organizational systems resulting in the unauthorized disclosure of CUI.

3.1.15 Authorize remote execution of privileged commands and remote access to security-relevant information.

Privileged commands give individuals the ability to execute sensitive, security-critical, or security-relevant system functions. Controlling such access from remote locations helps to ensure that unauthorized individuals are not able to execute such commands freely with the potential to do serious or catastrophic damage to organizational systems.

3.1.16 Authorize wireless access prior to allowing such connections.

Establishing usage restrictions and configuration/connection requirements for wireless access to the system provides criteria for organizations to support wireless access authorization decisions. Such restrictions and requirements reduce the susceptibility to unauthorized access to the system through wireless technologies.

3.1.17 Protect wireless access using authentication and encryption.

Organizations authenticate individuals and devices to help protect wireless access to the system. Special attention is given to the wide variety of devices that are part of the Internet of Things with potential wireless access to organizational systems.

3.1.18 Control connection of mobile devices.

Due to the large variety of mobile devices with different technical characteristics and capabilities, organizational restrictions may vary for the different types of devices. Usage restrictions and implementation guidance for mobile devices include: device identification and authentication; configuration management; implementation of mandatory protective software (e.g., malicious code detection, firewall); scanning devices for malicious code; updating virus protection software; scanning for critical software updates and patches; conducting primary operating system (and possibly other resident software) integrity checks; and disabling unnecessary hardware (e.g., wireless, infrared).

3.1.19 Encrypt CUI on mobile devices and mobile computing platforms.

Organizations can employ full-device encryption or container-based encryption to protect the confidentiality of CUI on mobile devices and computing platforms. Container-based encryption provides a more fine-grained approach to the encryption of data and information including encrypting selected data structures such as files, records, or fields.

3.1.20 Verify and control/limit connections to and use of external systems.

External systems are systems or components of systems for which organizations typically have no direct supervision and authority over the application of security requirements and controls or the determination of the effectiveness of implemented controls on those systems.

Organizations establish terms and conditions for the use of external systems in accordance with organizational security policies and procedures. Terms and conditions address as a minimum, the types of applications that can be accessed on organizational systems from external systems. If terms and conditions with the owners of external systems cannot be established, organizations may impose restrictions on organizational personnel using those external systems.

3.1.21 Limit use of portable storage devices on external systems.

Limits on the use of organization-controlled portable storage devices in external systems include complete prohibition of the use of such devices or restrictions on how the devices may be used and under what conditions the devices may be used.

3.1.22 Control CUI posted or processed on publicly accessible systems.

In accordance with laws, Executive Orders, directives, policies, regulations, or standards, the public is not authorized access to nonpublic information (e.g., information protected under the Privacy Act, CUI, and proprietary information). This requirement addresses systems that are controlled by the organization and accessible to the public, typically without identification or authentication. The content of information is reviewed prior to posting onto publicly accessible systems to ensure that nonpublic information is not included.

2: Awareness and Training (AT)

Organizations must ensure that managers and users of organizational information systems are made aware of the security risks associated with their activities and of the applicable laws, Executive Orders, directives, policies, standards, instructions, regulations, or procedures related to the security of organizational information systems; and ensure that organizational personnel are adequately trained to carry out their assigned information security-related duties and responsibilities. In ISO 27001, training is covered in control A.7.2.2 of Annex A.

3.2 AWARENESS AND TRAINING

Basic Security Requirements

3.2.1 Ensure that managers, systems administrators, and users of organizational systems are made aware of the security risks associated with their activities and of the applicable policies, standards, and procedures related to the security of those systems.

Organizations determine the content and frequency of security awareness training and security awareness … The content includes a basic understanding of the need for information security and user actions to maintain security and to respond to suspected security incidents. The content also addresses awareness of the need for operations security. Security awareness techniques include: formal training; offering supplies inscribed with security reminders; generating email advisories or notices from organizational officials; displaying logon screen messages; displaying security awareness posters; and conducting information security awareness events.

3.2.2 Ensure that personnel are trained to carry out their assigned information security-related duties and responsibilities.

Comprehensive role-based training addresses management, operational, and technical roles and responsibilities covering physical, personnel, and technical controls. Such training can include policies, procedures, tools, and artifacts for the security roles defined. Organizations also provide the training necessary for individuals to carry out their responsibilities related to operations and supply chain security within the context of organizational information security programs.

3.2.3 Provide security awareness training on recognizing and reporting potential indicators of insider threat.

Security awareness training includes how to communicate employee and management concerns regarding potential indicators of insider threat through appropriate organizational channels in accordance with established organizational policies and procedures. Organizations may consider tailoring insider threat awareness topics to the role (e.g., training for managers may be focused on specific changes in behavior of team members, while training for employees may be focused on more general observations).

3: Audit and Accountability (AU)

Organizations must create, protect, and retain information system audit records to the extent needed to enable the monitoring, analysis, investigation, and reporting of unlawful, unauthorized, or inappropriate information system activity; and ensure that the actions of individual information system users can be uniquely traced to those users so they can be held accountable for their actions. Audit and accountability are also key to the ISO 27001 system, required by Clauses 9.2 and 9.3 of the Standard and protection of records is required by A.18.1.3.

3.3 AUDIT AND ACCOUNTABILITY

Basic Security Requirements

3.3.1 Create and retain system audit logs and records to the extent needed to enable the monitoring, analysis, investigation, and reporting of unlawful or unauthorized system activity.

Organizations identify event types for which a logging functionality is needed as those events which are significant and relevant to the security of systems and the environments in which those systems operate to meet specific and ongoing auditing needs.

… Audit logs are reviewed and analyzed as often as needed to provide important information to organizations to facilitate risk-based decision making.

3.3.2 Ensure that the actions of individual system users can be uniquely traced to those users, so they can be held accountable for their actions.

This requirement ensures that the contents of the audit record include the information needed to link the audit event to the actions of an individual to the extent feasible.

3.3.3 Review and update logged events

Reviewing and updating the set of logged event types periodically is necessary to ensure that the current set remains necessary and sufficient.

3.3.4 Alert in the event of an audit logging process failure.

Audit logging process failures include software and hardware errors, failures in the audit record capturing mechanisms, and audit record storage capacity being reached or exceeded.

3.3.5 Correlate audit record review, analysis, and reporting processes for investigation and response to indications of unlawful, unauthorized, suspicious, or unusual activity.

Correlating audit record review, analysis, and reporting processes helps to ensure that they do not operate independently, but rather collectively.

3.3.6 Provide audit record reduction and report generation to support on-demand analysis and reporting.

Audit record reduction is a process that manipulates collected audit information and organizes such information in a summary format that is more meaningful to analysts … Audit record reduction capability can include, for example, modern data mining techniques with advanced data filters to identify anomalous behavior in audit records.

3.3.7 Provide a system capability that compares and synchronizes internal system clocks with an authoritative source to generate time stamps for audit records.

Internal system clocks are used to generate time stamps, which include date and time … This requirement provides uniformity of time stamps for systems with multiple system clocks and systems connected over a network.

3.3.8 Protect audit information and audit logging tools from unauthorized access, modification, and deletion.

This requirement focuses on the technical protection of audit information and limits the ability to access and execute audit logging tools to authorized individuals. Physical protection of audit information is addressed by media protection and physical and environmental protection requirements.

3.3.9 Limit management of audit logging functionality to a subset of privileged users.

Individuals with privileged access to a system and who are also the subject of an audit by that system, may affect the reliability of audit information by inhibiting audit logging activities or modifying audit records. This requirement specifies that privileged access be further defined between audit-related privileges and other privileges, thus limiting the users with audit-related privileges.

4: Configuration Management (CM)

Organizations must "Establish and maintain baseline configurations and inventories of organizational systems (including hardware, software, firmware, and documentation) throughout the respective system development life cycles"[35] and "Establish and enforce security configuration settings for

---

[35] NIST SP 800-171 Rev. 2: 3.4.1.

information technology products employed in organizational systems."[36] Inventories play a role in several parts of the ISO 27001 process. The most similar requirement is Annex A control A.8, but an in-depth asset inventory may be part of the risk assessment process in Clause 6.1.2. Baseline configurations are part of the implementation process. Configuration management is part of the implementation of Annex A control A.12 with reference to ISO 27002, the supplementary standard that provides advice on how to implement the Annex A security controls.

3.4 CONFIGURATION MANAGEMENT

Basic Security Requirements

3.4.1 Establish and maintain baseline configurations and inventories of organizational systems (including hardware, software, firmware, and documentation) throughout the respective system development life cycles.

Organizations can implement centralized system component inventories that include components from multiple organizational systems. In such situations, organizations ensure that the resulting inventories include system-specific information required for proper component accountability (e.g., system association, system owner).

3.4.2 Establish and enforce security configuration settings for information technology products employed in organizational systems.

Common secure configurations (also referred to as security configuration checklists, lockdown and hardening guides, security reference guides, security technical implementation guides) provide recognized, standardized, and established benchmarks that stipulate secure configuration settings for specific information technology platforms/products and

---

[36] NIST SP 800-171 Rev. 2: 3.4.2.

instructions for configuring those system components to meet operational requirements.

3.4.3 Track, review, approve or disapprove, and log changes to organizational systems.

Tracking, reviewing, approving/disapproving, and logging changes is called configuration change control. Configuration change control for organizational systems involves the systematic proposal, justification, implementation, testing, review, and disposition of changes to the systems, including system upgrades and modifications.

3.4.4 Analyze the security impact of changes prior to implementation.

Security impact analysis may include reviewing security plans to understand security requirements and reviewing system design documentation to understand the implementation of controls and how specific changes might affect the controls. Security impact analyses may also include risk assessments to better understand the impact of the changes and to determine if additional controls are required.

3.4.5 Define, document, approve, and enforce physical and logical access restrictions associated with changes to organizational systems.

Access restrictions include physical and logical access control requirements, workflow automation, media libraries, abstract layers (e.g., changes implemented into external interfaces rather than directly into systems), and change windows (e.g., changes occur only during certain specified times).

3.4.6 Employ the principle of least functionality by configuring organizational systems to provide only essential capabilities.

Organizations review functions and services provided by systems or components of systems, to determine which functions and services are candidates for elimination. Organizations disable unused or unnecessary physical and logical ports and protocols to prevent unauthorized connection of devices, transfer of information, and tunneling.

3.4.7 Restrict, disable, or prevent the use of nonessential programs, functions, ports, protocols, and services.

Restricting the use of nonessential software (programs) includes restricting the roles allowed to approve program execution; prohibiting auto-execute; program blacklisting and whitelisting; or restricting the number of program instances executed at the same time. The organization makes a security-based determination which functions, ports, protocols, and/or services are restricted. Bluetooth, File Transfer Protocol (FTP), and peer-to-peer networking are examples of protocols organizations consider preventing the use of, restricting, or disabling.

3.4.8 Apply deny-by-exception (blacklisting) policy to prevent the use of unauthorized software or deny-all, permit-by-exception (whitelisting) policy to allow the execution of authorized software.

In addition to whitelisting, organizations consider verifying the integrity of whitelisted software programs using, for example, cryptographic checksums, digital signatures, or hash functions. Verification of whitelisted software can occur either prior to execution or at system start-up.

3.4.9 Control and monitor user-installed software.

Users can install software in organizational systems if provided the necessary privileges. To maintain control over the software installed, organizations identify permitted and prohibited actions regarding software installation through policies. Permitted software installations include updates and security patches to existing software and applications from organization-approved "app stores."

5: Identification and Authentication (IA)

Organizations must identify information system users, processes acting on behalf of users, or devices and authenticate (or verify) the identities of those users, processes, or devices, as a prerequisite to allowing access to organizational information systems. Identification and authentication are part of the access control determined in ISO 27001 Annex A control set A.9.

3.5 IDENTIFICATION AND AUTHENTICATION

Basic Security Requirements

3.5.1 Identify system users, processes acting on behalf of users, and devices.

Common device identifiers include Media Access Control (MAC), Internet Protocol (IP) addresses, or device-unique token identifiers. Management of individual identifiers is not applicable to shared system accounts. Typically, individual identifiers are the usernames associated with the system accounts assigned to those individuals.

3.5.2 Authenticate (or verify) the identities of users, processes, or devices, as a prerequisite to allowing access to organizational systems.

Individual authenticators include the following: passwords, key cards, cryptographic devices, and one-time password devices … Developers ship system components with factory default authentication credentials to allow for initial installation and configuration. Default authentication credentials are often well known, easily discoverable, and present a significant security risk.

Systems support authenticator management by organization-defined settings and restrictions for various authenticator characteristics including minimum password length, validation time window for time synchronous one-time tokens, and number of allowed rejections during the verification stage of biometric authentication.

3.5.3 Use multifactor authentication for local and network access to privileged accounts and for network access to non-privileged accounts.

Multifactor authentication requires the use of two or more different factors to authenticate. The factors are defined as something you know (e.g., password, personal identification number [PIN]); something you have (e.g., cryptographic identification device, token); or something you are (e.g., biometric).

Before using biometric information that can be stored, review local privacy laws like the GDPR or the Illinois Biometric Information Protection Act.

3.5.4 Employ replay-resistant authentication mechanisms for network access to privileged and non-privileged accounts.

Authentication processes resist replay attacks if it is impractical to successfully authenticate by recording or replaying previous authentication messages. Replay-resistant techniques include protocols that use nonces or challenges such as time synchronous or challenge-response one-time authenticators.

3.5.5 Prevent reuse of identifiers for a defined period.

Identifiers are provided for users, processes acting on behalf of users, or devices (3.5.1). Preventing reuse of identifiers implies preventing the assignment of previously used individual, group, role, or device identifiers to different individuals, groups, roles, or devices.

3.5.6 Disable identifiers after a defined period of inactivity.

Inactive identifiers pose a risk to organizational information because attackers may exploit an inactive identifier to gain undetected access to organizational devices. The owners of the inactive accounts may not notice if unauthorized access to the account has been obtained.

3.5.7 Enforce a minimum password complexity and change of characters when new passwords are created.

This requirement applies to single-factor authentication of individuals using passwords as individual or group authenticators, and in a similar manner, when passwords are used as part of multifactor authenticators. The number of changed characters refers to the number of changes required with respect to the total number of positions in the current password. To mitigate certain brute force attacks against passwords, organizations may also consider salting passwords.

3.5.8 Prohibit password reuse for a specified number of generations.

Password lifetime restrictions do not apply to temporary passwords.

3.5.9 Allow temporary password use for system logons with an immediate change to a permanent password.

Changing temporary passwords to permanent passwords immediately after system logon ensures that the necessary strength of the authentication mechanism is implemented at the earliest opportunity, reducing the susceptibility to authenticator compromises.

3.5.10 Store and transmit only cryptographically-protected passwords.

Cryptographically-protected passwords use salted one-way cryptographic hashes of passwords.

3.5.11 Obscure feedback of authentication information.

The feedback from systems does not provide any information that would allow unauthorized individuals to compromise authentication mechanisms. For some types of systems or system components, for example, desktop or notebook computers with relatively large monitors, the threat (often referred to as shoulder surfing) may be significant. For other types of systems or components, for example, mobile devices with small displays, this threat may be less significant.

6: Incident Response (IR)

Organizations must establish an operational incident handling capability for organizational information systems that includes adequate preparation, detection, analysis, containment, recovery, and user response activities; and track, document, and report incidents to appropriate organizational officials and/or authorities. Information security incident management is considered in ISO 27001 Annex A control set A.16.

3.6 INCIDENT RESPONSE

Basic Security Requirements

3.6.1 Establish an operational incident-handling capability for organizational systems that includes preparation, detection, analysis, containment, recovery, and user response activities.

Incident-related information can be obtained from a variety of sources including audit monitoring, network monitoring, physical access monitoring, user and administrator reports, and reported supply chain events. Effective incident handling capability includes coordination among many organizational entities including mission/business owners, system owners, authorizing officials, human resources offices, physical and personnel security offices, legal departments, operations personnel, procurement offices, and the risk executive.

As part of user response activities, incident response training is provided by organizations and is linked directly to the assigned roles and responsibilities of organizational personnel to ensure that the appropriate content and level of detail is included in such training.

3.6.2 Track, document, and report incidents to designated officials and/or authorities both internal and external to the organization.

Tracking and documenting system security incidents includes maintaining records about each incident, the status of the incident, and other pertinent information necessary for forensics, evaluating incident details, trends, and handling ... Reporting incidents addresses specific incident reporting requirements within an organization and the formal incident reporting requirements for the organization.

3.6.3 Test the organizational incident response capability.

Organizations test incident response capabilities to determine the effectiveness of the capabilities and to identify potential weaknesses or deficiencies. Incident response testing includes the use of checklists, walk-through or tabletop exercises, simulations (both parallel and full interrupt), and comprehensive exercises. Incident response testing can also include a determination of the effects on organizational operations (e.g., reduction in mission capabilities), organizational assets, and individuals due to incident response.

7: Maintenance (MA)

Organizations must perform periodic and timely maintenance on organizational information systems; and provide effective controls on the tools, techniques, mechanisms, and personnel used to conduct information system maintenance. Maintenance is covered in ISO 27001 Annex A control A.11.2.4.

3.7 MAINTENANCE

Basic Security Requirements

3.7.1 Perform maintenance on organizational systems.

Addresses the information security aspects of the system maintenance program and applies to all types of maintenance to any system component (including hardware, firmware, applications) conducted by any local or nonlocal entity. System maintenance also includes those components not directly associated with information processing and data or information retention such as scanners, copiers, and printers.

3.7.2 Provide controls on the tools, techniques, mechanisms, and personnel used to conduct system maintenance.

This requirement addresses security-related issues with maintenance tools that are not within the organizational system boundaries that process, store, or transmit CUI, but are used specifically for diagnostic and repair actions on those systems.

3.7.3 Ensure equipment removed for off-site maintenance is sanitized of any CUI.

This requirement addresses the information security aspects of system maintenance that are performed off-site and applies to all types of maintenance to any system component (including applications) conducted by a local or nonlocal entity (e.g., in-contract, warranty, in- house, software maintenance agreement).

3.7.4 Check media containing diagnostic and test programs for malicious code before the media are used in organizational systems.

If, upon inspection of media containing maintenance diagnostic and test programs, organizations determine that the media contain malicious code, the incident is handled consistent with incident handling policies and procedures.

3.7.5 Require multifactor authentication to establish nonlocal maintenance sessions via external network connections and terminate such connections when nonlocal maintenance is complete.

Nonlocal maintenance and diagnostic activities are those activities conducted by individuals communicating through an external network. The authentication techniques employed in the establishment of these nonlocal maintenance and diagnostic sessions reflect the network access requirements in 3.5.3.

3.7.6 Supervise the maintenance activities of maintenance personnel without required access authorization.

Individuals not previously identified as authorized maintenance personnel, such as information technology manufacturers, vendors, consultants, and systems integrators, may require privileged access to organizational systems, for example, when required to conduct maintenance activities with little or no notice. Organizations may choose to issue temporary credentials to these individuals based on organizational risk assessments. Temporary credentials may be for one-time use or for very limited time periods.

8: Media Protection (MP)

Organizations must protect information system media, both paper and digital; limit access to information on information system media to authorized users; and sanitize or destroy information system media before disposal or release for reuse. Media protection is considered in ISO 27001 Annex A control set A.11.

3.8 MEDIA PROTECTION

Basic Security Requirements

3.8.1 Protect (i.e., physically control and securely store) system media containing CUI, both paper and digital.

Protecting digital media includes limiting access to design specifications stored on compact disks or flash drives in the media library to the project leader and any individuals on the development team. Physically controlling system media includes conducting inventories, maintaining accountability for stored media, and ensuring procedures are in place to allow individuals to check out and return media to the media library.

3.8.2 Limit access to CUI on system media to authorized users.

Access can be limited by physically controlling system media and secure storage areas. Physically controlling system media includes conducting inventories, ensuring procedures are in place to allow individuals to check out and return system media to the media library, and maintaining accountability for all stored media. Secure storage includes a locked drawer, desk, or cabinet, or a controlled media library.

3.8.3 Sanitize or destroy system media containing CUI before disposal or release for reuse.

This requirement applies to all system media, digital and non-digital, subject to disposal or reuse … The sanitization process removes information from the media such that the information cannot be retrieved or reconstructed. Sanitization techniques, including clearing, purging, cryptographic erase, and destruction, prevent the disclosure of information to unauthorized individuals when such media is released for reuse or disposal.

3.8.4 Mark media with necessary CUI markings and distribution limitations.

The term security marking refers to the application or use of human-readable security attributes. System media includes digital and non-digital media. Marking of system media reflects applicable federal laws, Executive Orders, directives, policies, and regulations.

3.8.5 Control access to media containing CUI and maintain accountability for media during transport outside of controlled areas.

Controlled areas are areas or spaces for which organizations provide physical or procedural controls to meet the requirements established for protecting systems and information. Controls to maintain accountability for media during transport include locked containers and cryptography. Cryptographic mechanisms can provide confidentiality and integrity protections depending upon the mechanisms used.

3.8.6 Implement cryptographic mechanisms to protect the confidentiality of CUI stored on digital media during transport unless otherwise protected by alternative physical safeguards.

This requirement applies to portable storage devices (e.g., USB memory sticks, digital video disks, compact disks, external or removable hard disk drives).

3.8.7 Control the use of removable media on system components.

This requirement restricts the use of certain types of media on systems, for example, restricting or prohibiting the use of flash drives or external hard disk drives. Organizations can employ technical and nontechnical controls (e.g., policies, procedures, and rules of behavior) to control the use of system media.

3.8.8 Prohibit the use of portable storage devices when such devices have no identifiable owner.

Requiring identifiable owners (e.g., individuals, organizations, or projects) for portable storage devices reduces the overall risk of using such technologies by allowing organizations to assign responsibility and accountability for addressing known vulnerabilities in the devices (e.g., insertion of malicious code).

3.8.9 Protect the confidentiality of backup CUI at storage locations.

Organizations can employ cryptographic mechanisms or alternative physical controls to protect the confidentiality of backup information at designated storage locations. Backed-up information containing CUI may include system-level information and user-level information. System-level information includes system-state information, operating system software, application software, and licenses. User-level information includes information other than system-level information.

9: Personnel Security (PS)

Organizations must ensure that individuals occupying positions of responsibility within organizations (including third-party service providers) are trustworthy and meet established security criteria for those positions; ensure that organizational information and information systems are protected during and after personnel actions such as terminations and transfers; and employ formal sanctions for personnel failing to comply with organizational security policies and procedures. Most of the controls concerning personnel are considered ISO 27001 Annex A control set A.7, but some, like competence, are considered in Clause 7.2.

3.9 PERSONNEL SECURITY

Basic Security Requirements

3.9.1 Screen individuals prior to authorizing access to organizational systems containing CUI.

Personnel security screening (vetting) activities involve the evaluation/assessment of individual's conduct, integrity, judgment, loyalty, reliability, and stability (i.e., the trustworthiness of the individual) prior to authorizing access to organizational systems containing CUI. The screening activities reflect applicable federal laws, Executive Orders, directives, policies, regulations, and specific criteria established for the level of access required for assigned positions.

3.9.2 Ensure that organizational systems containing CUI are protected during and after personnel actions such as terminations and transfers.

Protecting CUI during and after personnel actions may include returning system-related property and conducting exit interviews. System-related property includes hardware authentication tokens, identification cards, system administration technical manuals, keys, and building passes. Exit interviews ensure that individuals who have been terminated understand the security constraints imposed by being former employees and that proper accountability is achieved for system-related property.

10: Physical and Environmental Protection (PE)

Organizations must limit physical access to information systems, equipment, and the respective operating environments to authorized individuals; protect the physical plant and support infrastructure for information systems; provide supporting utilities for information systems; protect information systems against environmental hazards; and provide appropriate environmental controls in facilities containing information systems. Physical and environmental security is considered in Annex A.11. This is one of the largest domains in Annex A. It includes two objectives and 15 controls. These are similar to the controls in this section or they can be implemented in ways that are equivalent.

3.10 PHYSICAL PROTECTION

Basic Security Requirements

3.10.1 Limit physical access to organizational systems, equipment, and the respective operating environments to authorized individuals.

This requirement applies to employees, individuals with permanent physical access authorization credentials, and visitors. Authorized individuals have credentials that include badges, identification cards, and smart cards.

3.10.2 Protect and monitor the physical facility and support infrastructure for organizational systems.

Monitoring of physical access includes publicly accessible areas within organizational facilities. This can be accomplished, for example, by the employment of guards; the use of sensor devices; or the use of video surveillance equipment such as cameras.

3.10.3 Escort visitors and monitor visitor activity.

Individuals with permanent physical access authorization credentials are not considered visitors. Audit logs can be used to monitor visitor activity.

3.10.4 Maintain audit logs of physical access

Organizations have flexibility in the types of audit logs employed. Audit logs can be procedural (e.g., a written log of individuals accessing the facility), automated (e.g., capturing ID provided by a PIV card), or some combination thereof.

3.10.5 Control and manage physical access devices.

Physical access devices include keys, locks, combinations, and card readers.

3.10.6 Enforce safeguarding measures for CUI at alternate work sites.

Alternate work sites may include government facilities or the private residences of employees. Organizations may define different security requirements for specific alternate work sites or types of sites depending on the work-related activities conducted at those sites.

11: Risk Assessment (RA)

Organizations must periodically assess the risk to organizational operations (including mission, functions, image, or reputation), organizational assets, and individuals, resulting from the operation of organizational information systems and the associated processing, storage, or transmission of organizational information. Risk assessment is one of the central parts of the ISO 27001 information security management system (ISMS). Part of the security architecture should be known in order for you to be able to understand your risks. Every firm is different and should provide resources appropriate to their risks. The risk assessment is not part of Annex A, it is part of ISO 27001 clause 6.1.2 and as such, it is mandatory. It also has to be reviewed at planned intervals or when there are changes.

3.11 RISK ASSESSMENT

Basic Security Requirements

3.11.1 Periodically assess the risk to organizational operations (including mission, functions, image, or reputation), organizational assets, and individuals, resulting from the operation of organizational systems and the associated processing, storage, or transmission of CUI.

Clearly defined system boundaries are a prerequisite for effective risk assessments. Such risk assessments consider threats, vulnerabilities, likelihood, and impact to organizational operations, organizational assets, and individuals based on the operation and use of organizational systems. Risk assessments also consider risk from external parties (e.g., service providers, contractors operating systems on behalf of the organization, individuals accessing organizational systems, outsourcing entities).

3.11.2 Scan for vulnerabilities in organizational systems and applications periodically and when new vulnerabilities affecting those systems and applications are identified.

Determine the required vulnerability scanning for all system components, ensuring that potential sources of vulnerabilities such as networked printers, scanners, and copiers are not overlooked.

3.11.3 Remediate vulnerabilities in accordance with risk assessments.

Vulnerabilities discovered, for example, via the scanning conducted in response to 3.11.2, are remediated with consideration of the related assessment of risk. The consideration of risk influences the prioritization of remediation efforts and the level of effort to be expended in the remediation for specific vulnerabilities.

12: Security Assessment (CA)

Are processes and procedures still effective? Are improvements needed? Organizations must allocate sufficient resources to adequately protect organizational information systems; employ system development life cycle processes that incorporate information security considerations; employ software usage and installation restrictions; and ensure that third-party providers employ adequate security measures to protect information, applications, and/or services outsourced from the organization. The ISO 27001 management system is really a process of continual improvement. One of the most important clauses is clause 9 which requires, like this domain, that the organization monitor the system, audit the system, review the audit and correct any problems.

3.12 SECURITY ASSESSMENT

Basic Security Requirements

3.12.1 Periodically assess the security controls in organizational systems to determine if the controls are effective in their application.

Organizations assess security controls in organizational systems and the environments in which those systems operate as part of the system development life cycle. Security controls are the safeguards or countermeasures organizations implement to satisfy security requirements. By assessing the implemented security controls, organizations determine if the security safeguards or countermeasures are in place and operating as intended.

3.12.2 Develop and implement plans of action designed to correct deficiencies and reduce or eliminate vulnerabilities in organizational systems.

The plan of action is a key document in the information security program. Organizations develop plans of action that describe how any unimplemented security requirements will be met and how any planned mitigations will be implemented. Organizations can document the system security plan and plan of action as separate or combined documents and in any chosen format.

3.12.3 Monitor security controls on an ongoing basis to ensure the continued effectiveness of the controls.

Continuous monitoring programs facilitate ongoing awareness of threats, vulnerabilities, and information security to support organizational risk management decisions. The terms continuous and ongoing imply that organizations assess and analyze security controls and information security-related risks at a frequency sufficient to support risk-based decisions.

3.12.4 Develop, document, and periodically update system security plans that describe system boundaries, system environments of operation, how security requirements are

implemented, and the relationships with or connections to other systems.

System security plans relate security requirements to a set of security controls. System security plans also describe, at a high level, how the security controls meet those security requirements, but do not provide detailed, technical descriptions of the design or implementation of the controls.

13: System and Communications Protection (SC)

Organizations must monitor, control, and protect organizational communications (i.e., information transmitted or received by organizational information systems) at the external boundaries and key internal boundaries of the information systems; and employ architectural designs, software development techniques, and systems engineering principles that promote effective information security within organizational information systems. The controls in this section are all in the ISO 27001 system, both the clauses and in the Annex A, but not in one place. An ISO 27001 adapted to CMMC implementation will require either specific adaptation of Annex A controls or the addition of extra controls to clearly demonstrate CMMC compliance.

3.13 SYSTEM AND COMMUNICATIONS PROTECTION

Basic Security Requirements

3.13.1 Monitor, control, and protect communications (i.e., information transmitted or received by organizational systems) at the external boundaries and key internal boundaries of organizational systems.

Communications can be monitored, controlled, and protected at boundary components and by restricting or prohibiting interfaces in organizational systems. Boundary components include gateways, routers, firewalls, guards, network-based malicious code analysis and virtualization systems, or encrypted tunnels implemented within a system security architecture (e.g., routers protecting firewalls or application gateways residing on protected subnetworks).

3.13.2 Employ architectural designs, software development techniques, and systems engineering principles that promote effective information security within organizational systems.

Organizations apply systems security engineering principles to new development systems or systems undergoing major upgrades. For legacy systems, organizations apply systems security engineering principles to system upgrades and modifications to the extent feasible, given the current state of hardware, software, and firmware components within those systems.

3.13.3 Separate user functionality from system management functionality.

System management functionality includes functions necessary to administer databases, network components, workstations, or servers, and typically requires privileged user access. The separation of user functionality from system management functionality is physical or logical.

3.13.4 Prevent unauthorized and unintended information transfer via shared system resources.

The control of information in shared system resources (e.g., registers, cache memory, main memory, hard disks) is also commonly referred to as object reuse and residual information protection. This requirement prevents information produced by the actions of prior users or roles … from being available to any current users or roles.

3.13.5 Implement subnetworks for publicly accessible system components that are physically or logically separated from internal networks.

Subnetworks that are physically or logically separated from internal networks are referred to as demilitarized zones (DMZs). DMZs are typically implemented with boundary control devices and techniques that include routers, gateways, firewalls, virtualization, or cloud-based technologies.

3.13.6 Deny network communications traffic by default and allow network communications traffic by exception (i.e., deny all, permit by exception).

This requirement applies to inbound and outbound network communications traffic at the system boundary and at identified points within the system. A deny-all, permit-by-exception network communications traffic policy ensures that only those connections which are essential and approved are allowed.

3.13.7 Prevent remote devices from simultaneously establishing non-remote connections with organizational systems and communicating via some other connection to resources in external networks (i.e., split tunneling).

This requirement is implemented in remote devices (e.g., notebook computers, smart phones, and tablets) through configuration settings to disable split tunneling in those devices, and by preventing configuration settings from being readily configurable by users. This requirement is implemented in the system by the detection of split tunneling (or of configuration settings that allow split tunneling) in the remote device, and by prohibiting the connection if the remote device is using split tunneling.

3.13.8 Implement cryptographic mechanisms to prevent unauthorized disclosure of CUI during transmission unless otherwise protected by alternative physical safeguards.

This requirement applies to internal and external networks and any system components that can transmit information including servers, notebook computers, desktop computers, mobile devices, printers, copiers, scanners, and facsimile machines.

3.13.9 Terminate network connections associated with communications sessions at the end of the sessions or after a defined period of inactivity.

This requirement applies to internal and external networks. Terminating network connections associated with communications sessions include de-allocating associated TCP/IP address or port pairs at the operating system level.

3.13.10 Establish and manage cryptographic keys for cryptography employed in organizational systems.

Cryptographic key management and establishment can be performed using manual procedures or mechanisms supported by manual procedures. Organizations define key management requirements in accordance with applicable federal laws, Executive Orders, policies, directives, regulations, and standards specifying appropriate options, levels, and parameters.

3.13.11 Employ FIPS-validated cryptography when used to protect the confidentiality of CUI.

Cryptography can be employed to support many security solutions including the protection of controlled unclassified information, the provision of digital signatures, and the enforcement of information separation ... Cryptography can also be used to support random number generation and hash generation. Cryptographic standards include FIPS-validated cryptography and/or NSA-approved cryptography.

3.13.12 Prohibit remote activation of collaborative computing devices and provide indication of devices in use to users present at the device.

Collaborative computing devices include networked white boards, cameras, and microphones. Indication of use includes signals to users when collaborative computing devices are activated. Dedicated video conferencing systems, which rely on one of the participants calling or connecting to the other party to activate the video conference, are excluded.

3.13.13 Control and monitor the use of mobile code.

Mobile code technologies include Java, JavaScript, ActiveX, Postscript, PDF, Flash animations, and VBScript. Decisions regarding the use of mobile code in organizational systems are based on the potential for the code to cause damage to the systems if used maliciously. Usage restrictions and implementation guidance apply to the selection and use of mobile code installed on servers and mobile code downloaded and executed on individual workstations, notebook computers, and devices (e.g., smart phones). Mobile code policy and procedures address controlling or preventing the development, acquisition, or introduction of unacceptable mobile code in systems, including requiring mobile code to be digitally signed by a trusted source.

3.13.14 Control and monitor the use of Voice over Internet Protocol (VoIP) technologies.

To address the threats associated with VoIP, usage restrictions and implementation guidelines are based on the potential for the VoIP technology to cause damage to the system if it is used maliciously. Threats to VoIP are similar to those inherent with any Internet-based application.

3.13.15 Protect the authenticity of communications sessions.

Authenticity protection includes protecting against man-in-the-middle attacks, session hijacking, and the insertion of false information into communications sessions. This requirement addresses communications protection at the session versus packet level (e.g., sessions in service-oriented architectures providing web-based services) and establishes grounds for confidence at both ends of communications sessions in ongoing identities of other parties and in the validity of information transmitted.

3.13.16 Protect the confidentiality of CUI at rest.

Organizations can use different mechanisms to achieve confidentiality protections, including the use of cryptographic mechanisms and file share scanning. Organizations may also use other controls including secure off-line storage in lieu of online storage when adequate protection of information at rest cannot otherwise be achieved or continuous monitoring to identify malicious code at rest.

14: System and Information Integrity (SI)

Organizations must identify, report, and correct information and information system flaws in a timely manner; provide protection from malicious code at appropriate locations within organizational information systems; and monitor information system security alerts and advisories and take appropriate actions in response. One of the key benefits of ISO 270001 is continual improvement. The requirements found in Clause 9.1, 9.2 and 9.3 state that ISO 27001 certified firms must monitor, audit and review their systems at regular intervals. These reviews must be carried out by senior management and any flaws are required to be corrected.

3.14.1 Identify, report, and correct system flaws in a timely manner.

Organizations identify systems that are affected by announced software and firmware flaws including potential vulnerabilities resulting from those flaws and report this information to designated personnel with information security responsibilities. Security-relevant updates include patches, service packs, hot fixes, and anti-virus signatures.

3.14.2 Provide protection from malicious code at designated locations within organizational systems.

Designated locations include system entry and exit points which may include firewalls, remote-access servers, workstations, electronic mail servers, web servers, proxy servers, notebook computers, and mobile devices ... Malicious code protection mechanisms include anti-virus signature definitions and reputation-based technologies. A variety of technologies and methods exist to limit or eliminate the effects of malicious code.

3.14.3 Monitor system security alerts and advisories and take action in response.

There are many publicly available sources of system security alerts and advisories. For example, the Department of Homeland Security's Cybersecurity and Infrastructure Security Agency (CISA) generates security alerts and advisories to maintain situational awareness across the federal government and in nonfederal organizations.

3.14.4 Update malicious code protection mechanisms when new releases are available.

Malicious code protection mechanisms include anti-virus signature definitions and reputation-based technologies ... Traditional malicious code protection mechanisms cannot always detect such code. In these situations, organizations rely instead on other safeguards including secure coding practices, configuration management and control, trusted procurement processes, and monitoring practices to help ensure that software does not perform functions other than the functions intended.

3.14.5 Perform periodic scans of organizational systems and real-time scans of files from external sources as files are downloaded, opened, or executed.

Periodic scans of organizational systems and real-time scans of files from external sources can detect malicious code ... Malicious code can be inserted into systems in a variety of ways including web accesses, electronic mail, electronic mail attachments, and portable storage devices. Malicious code insertions occur through the exploitation of system vulnerabilities.

3.14.6 Monitor organizational systems, including inbound and outbound communications traffic, to detect attacks and indicators of potential attacks.

System monitoring includes external and internal monitoring. External monitoring includes the observation of events occurring at the system boundary (i.e., part of perimeter defense and boundary protection). Internal monitoring includes the observation of events occurring within the system.

3.14.7 Identify unauthorized use of organizational systems.

System monitoring can detect unauthorized use of organizational systems. System monitoring is an integral part of continuous monitoring and incident response programs. Monitoring is achieved through a variety of tools and techniques (e.g., intrusion detection systems, intrusion prevention systems, malicious code protection software, scanning tools, audit record monitoring software, network monitoring software).

The three additional domains in the CMMC

For the CMMC, the DoD added 3 more domains to the 14 taken from NIST SP 800-171. There are other frameworks with more exacting controls and, of course, one can always refer to NIST SP 800-53 Rev. 4 for the full catalog. The three additional controls will most likely be required for the higher levels of certification (levels 2 and above). The controls are:

15: Asset Management (AM)

This domain adds 14 additional controls. All of these controls are focused on the creation, protection and review of logs. As the level of certification increases from level 2 to level 5, the controls grow in sophistication and frequency of the log monitoring process. For example, at level 2, OSC are required to review audit logs. At level 4, the review should be automated.

These controls map to various controls in ISO 27001 Annex A, specifically the A.12.4 controls, as well as controls SI-11 and RA-5 in NIST SP 800-53 Rev. 4.

16: Situational Awareness (SA)

This domain has three controls – one at level 3, and two at level 4. These controls are concerned with threat hunting. They include a control for continuing contact with information sharing forums like the US-Cert at level 3.[37] Level 4 requires threat hunting capabilities that are designed to detect, track and disrupt threats that evade existing controls. NIST SP 800-53 Rev. 4 does not have a specific domain for SA. There is a domain for system information and integrity (SI) that contains some controls that refer to SA.

For example, the control Information System Monitoring SI-4 requires the organization to correlate information from monitoring tools employed throughout the information system in order to achieve organization-wide situational awareness. It

---

[37] *https://us-cert.cisa.gov/*.

also requires the organization to correlate results from monitoring physical, cyber and supply chain activities to achieve integrated SA. Similar cyber threat hunting capability controls can be found in NIST SP 800-172 3.11.3e, 3.14.1e, NIST SP 800-53 Rev. 4 SI-7 (1,6,9,10) and Annex A.6.1.3 and A.12.2.1.

17: Recovery (RE)

This domain requires four new controls centered around backup requirements. At different levels the requirement for backups become increasingly defined by larger scope, increased resiliency and availability. These requirements are similar to those found in NIST SP 800-53 Rev. 4 CP-9 and ISO 27001 Annex A 12.3.

CHAPTER 5: THE ROAD TO CERTIFICATION

Gap analysis and POA&Ms

Even the most cursory perusal of the 17 domains makes it obvious that implementing the controls is a long, involved process. Therefore, while the implementation of a NIST framework to protect CUI will undoubtedly increase cybersecurity manyfold for any organization, it should only be undertaken as a business decision. If the organization can exist and prosper only by fulfilling DoD contracts, then it should start the implementation process. It should be noted that this framework may be expanded to all government contracts that concern CUI. Since there are 70 CUI categories, the number of contracts where the implementation of these controls might be appropriate may be extensive.

The first step in the process is to determine where the gaps are in an organization's cybersecurity infrastructure. Even if an organization has little or no experience in building a cybersecurity system, this does not mean it does not have one. Every Windows 10 system comes with Windows Security, which includes automatic patching. Microsoft Defender can be enabled. Most mobile telephones are password protected and have a remote wipe feature.

A gap analysis is an assessment of an organization's cyber security profile that helps identify areas that need to be addressed. It is not just CMMC compliance – organizations may need certain controls because of contractual requirements. One of the most common is PCI DSS, an information security standard for organizations that handle credit cards payments and/or process, transmit, or store cardholder data. The number of controls required by the Standard is determined, like the CMMC, on a sliding scale. Since one of the easiest ways to hack any organization is through its suppliers, many organizations have other contractual requirement for their vendors.

There are other requirements. In the US, for example, organizations involved or affiliated with health care may be subject to the Health Insurance Portability and Accountability Act (HIPAA). Financial organizations may be subject to requirements of the Financial Industry Regulatory Authority (FINRA), and organizations listed on an exchange in the US will be subject to Securities Exchange Commission requirements. It is important when implementing a cybersecurity system that it integrates all the relevant requirements from these different regulators.

Then there are the various privacy laws. With the recent Schrems II decision, US organizations conducting business in the EU will find it increasingly difficult to comply with the GDPR.[38] Additionally, firms may have to comply with the California Consumer Privacy Act (CCPA), or even the California Privacy Rights Act (CPRA) if the California ballot initiative passes on November 3, 2020. It is also likely that the US will have some sort of federal privacy law similar to the GDPR within the next few years.

Besides contracts and regulation, an organization has to consider its own environment. What type(s) of data does it hold? Data about personal health? Financial data? CUI? Not all data presents the same risk – a lot of data, like the inventory of my garage, has little to no value, so it is not a good strategy to spend a lot of your cybersecurity budget to protect it. The allocation should be driven by the risk.

This process in the CMMC world is known as the Plan of Action and Milestones (POA&M). This is a term that originated with the US military and is defined as a document that identifies tasks needing to be accomplished. It details resources required to

---

[38] On July 16 2020, The European Court of Justice invalidated the EU-US Privacy Shield. For more information, see: *www.itgovernanceusa.com/blog/us-organizations-in-limbo-after-privacy-shield-is-invalidated*.

accomplish the elements of the plan, any milestones in meeting the tasks, and scheduled completion dates for the milestones.

Like a gap analysis, the purpose of the POA&M is to help organizations identify, assess, prioritize, and monitor the progress of corrective efforts for security weaknesses, deficiencies, or vulnerabilities in programs and systems assessments. The POA&M should create a disciplined and structured approach to mitigating risks in accordance with the priorities of the organization.

The POA&M is similar to the quality control process in ISO 27001. The Standard requires a risk assessment, which set the priorities. To address the risks, it requires a plan called the Statement of Applicability, which lists the 114 controls in the 14 categories of ISO 27001 Annex A.

Unlike NIST SP 800-171, ISO standards give the organization the choice to implement a control based on its need. ISO also encourages the organization to choose any additional controls that it believes could help increase the organization's cybersecurity posture. For example, some of these controls might include controls for the protection of Cloud or Internet of Things (IoT) utilization.

Both the POA&M and ISO 27001 processes are designed to be ongoing, learning processes to improve the quality of the organization's cybersecurity. To that end, the organization must regularly perform risk/security assessments of the information security system; as each assessment defines different risks, weaknesses or vulnerabilities, the system is incrementally improved.

Implementation

Once you determine what you need, you have to implement it. This is basically a three-step process.

Many organizations have many controls, but no documentation. They don't see the need. From their perspective, they know how to configure the firewall, so why should they write it down?

The first – and best – reason is that they are going to have to prove to a CMMC auditor that they know how to configure the firewall. According to Singapore's Personal Data Protection Commission;

> While an organization may have data protection policies and practices in place, it is equally pertinent that these policies are clearly documented. If an organization's policies and practices are not clearly documented and is simply a corporate practice / tradition e.g. through custom or verbal instructions, it would inevitably be difficult to demonstrate compliance.[39]

CMMC auditors will require an organization to demonstrate compliance.

The next step is to actually implement the control. This could be as simple as hiring a company to do pre-employment checks. It could also be more complicated, such as designing and implementing a security information and event management (SIEM) solution. Labeling and classifying assets may be necessary to determine what assets and information you have, but it certainly isn't something everyone enjoys. Building a good system takes a lot of work, money, and time, but if there is a business reason for doing it, the process will be worth it.

The final step, which is often ignored, is training. This means everyone in the organization, as all staff are responsible for cybersecurity. The fastest and easiest way to break into any organization's system is through its employees. People are the weakest link in the chain. Developing a sophisticated technical zero-day attack can take a long time and require lots of expensive resources. Criminal hackers can achieve the same in less time and at lower cost with a well-crafted, carefully targeted, and well-timed phishing email. Implementing and

---

[39] *www.jdsupra.com/legalnews/personal-data-protection-act-need-to-86759/.*

documenting is not sufficient, you have to walk the walk and talk the talk.

Audit

Once all the pieces are in place, it is time for the audit and this requires a CA. The CA could work independently or with a C3PAO. The CMMC-AB has made it easy to find/select an assessor by setting up a portal, CMMC Marketplace, to connect government contractors with qualified service providers.[40] The portal enables organizations to select a professional based on the organization's needs, its area of business, and the specific contract that it intends to bid for. Remember that CAs are qualified for different levels. If you need to be certified to level 5 you cannot use a CA who is only certified to level 3. You may also have to consider experience with certain types of businesses. For example, medical device regulation will require a different expertise than aircraft manufacturing. Your business might be only in the US or it could be global. It is far better to hire an assessor who has experience with your type of business, your interested parties, and your external or internal issues.

Once you find a suitable CA, the audit can begin. If the CA is satisfied, they will recommend certification. If they find any issues with the implementation, these problems have to be solved before certification can be issued. The organization seeking certification has up to 90 days to resolve the issue with the CA or their C3PAO.

Certification

Keep in mind that even if your CA is willing to approve certification, it does not mean you will be certified. Only the CMMC-AB can approve the assessment.

After any issues have been resolved, the CA will submit the assessment to the CMMC-AB. The assessment will then be reviewed by CMMC-AB QAs. If their review is satisfactory, the

---

[40] For more information, see: *www.cmmcab.org/marketplace*.

CMMC-AB can issue the certification. Certification is valid for up to three years and allows the organization to bid on any DoD contract up to the maturity level specified in the contract.

Cost

How much is all of this going to cost? Like anything else, it depends. It depends on the maturity of your system, and it depends on what maturity level you are trying to achieve. It depends on the size and complexity of your organization. Organizations conducting business in areas that are heavily regulated would be more challenging and more expensive to certify than simpler lines of business. However, there are three basic categories of costs:

1. The first category has to do with the cost of the expertise to prepare for audit. This involves consultants establishing the security of your systems with a gap analysis or POA&M. It is similar to an ISO 27001 gap analysis, which [generally costs $15,000–$35,000, is comparable to an ISO 27001 gap assessment]. If the systems are less mature, [$10,000–$25,000] is a reasonable estimate. If you don't have an up-to-date risk assessment and information security management system plan, you don't have a mature environment.

2. The second category of costs relates to the controls you need to implement to achieve certification. These could be as simple as drafting policies and procedures, or as complicated as implementing a SIEM solution or two-factor authentication. If you have not made a significant investment in the past five years, you should expect to pay between $5,000 and $70,000 to implement these systems. Again, it depends what you start with, what you do, and what you are trying to achieve. If you have been investing in your cybersecurity system or, for example, are already

ISO 27001 certified, the costs will be far smaller than if you are starting from scratch.

3.   The third category has to do with the costs associated with the certification audit itself. This is a fully defined audit program including interviews, gathering artefacts, samples, and a prescribed reporting format. Assuming the audit program follows a model of this nature, the pricing across auditors should be fairly consistent, with estimates of $20,000–$40,000.

The good news is that the cost of the CMMC audit might be considered an "allowable expense" or a reimbursable expense under FAR 52.216-7.[41] This means that DoD contractors will now be able to get reimbursement for CMMC preparation and assessment services as well as the remediation work that needs to be done to meet the appropriate level of cybersecurity controls specified in each contract.

---

[41] For more information, see the following article: "What Does It Mean When FAR 52.216-7 Is In Your Contract?", *www.mcnewassociates.com/what-does-it-mean-when-far-52-216-7-is-in-your-contract/*.

CHAPTER 6: CMMC IMPLICATIONS

At this time, it is hard to estimate the total implications of the CMMC program. The CMMC concerns annual contracts for the US military budget, which for the 2020 fiscal year, ran to $738 billion.[42] This covers about 350,000 contractors worldwide. The requirements of the CMMC are expected to be standard by 2026.

However, the program is unlikely to stop there. Cybersecurity is not just for the DoD. There are more than 70 categories of CUI, covering finance, immigration, natural and cultural resources, intellectual property, taxation, transportation, and more, all of which have government contractors or subcontractors. It is conceivable, perhaps even likely, that other executive branches could adopt the CMMC standard.

Partners, contractors, vendors, and customers all share information, and it only takes one weak link to compromise systems. Adoption of the CMMC could go way beyond what is required by the government and become standard for all organisations.

The problem is that many aspects of these programs are unknown and will not be known for a number of years. In the meantime, the best preparation is to certify to ISO 27001. ISO 27001 certification can be adapted to be almost identical to NIST SP 800-171. When more information about CMMC implementation is available, it is a simple task to tweak the ISO compliance to whatever is necessary.

The CMMC certification process is long and complicated, and is sure to be expensive. But the cost of poor cybersecurity is even greater. The best strategy is to start now and be ready for whatever eventually is adopted.

---

[42] www.cnbc.com/2019/12/21/trump-signs-738-billion-defense-bill.html.

FURTHER READING

IT Governance Publishing (ITGP) is the world's leading publisher for governance and compliance. Our industry-leading pocket guides, books, training resources, and toolkits are written by real-world practitioners and thought leaders. They are used globally by audiences of all levels, from students to C-suite executives.

Our high-quality publications cover all IT governance, risk, and compliance frameworks, and are available in a range of formats. This ensures our customers can access the information they need in the way they need it.

Other publications you may find useful include:

- *NIST Cybersecurity Framework – A pocket guide* by Alan Calder, *www.itgovernancepublishing.co.uk/product/nist-cybersecurity-framework*
- *Information Security Risk Management for ISO 27001/ISO 27002, third edition* by Alan Calder and Steve Watkins, *www.itgovernancepublishing.co.uk/product/information-security-risk-management-for-iso-27001-iso-27002-third-edition*
- *The California Consumer Privacy Act (CCPA) – An implementation guide* by Preston Bukaty, *www.itgovernancepublishing.co.uk/product/the-california-consumer-privacy-act-ccpa*

For more information on ITGP and branded publishing services, and to view our full list of publications, visit *www.itgovernancepublishing.co.uk*.

To receive regular updates from ITGP, including information on new publications in your area(s) of interest, sign up for our

newsletter:
www.itgovernancepublishing.co.uk/topic/newsletter.

Branded publishing

Through our branded publishing service, you can customize ITGP publications with your organization's branding.

Find out more at
www.itgovernancepublishing.co.uk/topic/branded-publishing-services.

Related services

ITGP is part of GRC International Group, which offers a comprehensive range of complementary products and services to help organizations meet their objectives.

For a full range of resources on the CMMC visit
www.itgovernanceusa.com/cybersecurity-maturity-model-certification.

Training services

The IT Governance training program is built on our extensive practical experience designing and implementing management systems based on ISO standards, best practice, and regulations.

Our courses help attendees develop practical skills and comply with contractual and regulatory requirements. They also support career development via recognized qualifications.

Learn more about our training courses and view the full course catalog at *www.itgovernanceusa.com/training*.

Professional services and consultancy

We are a leading global consultancy of IT governance, risk management, and compliance solutions. We advise organizations around the world on their most critical issues, and present cost-saving and risk-reducing solutions based on international best practice and frameworks.

We offer a wide range of delivery methods to suit all budgets, timescales, and preferred project approaches.

Find out how our consultancy services can help your organization at *www.itgovernanceusa.com/consulting*.

Industry news

Want to stay up to date with the latest developments and resources in the IT governance and compliance market? Subscribe to our Daily Sentinel newsletter and we will send you mobile-friendly emails with fresh news and features about your preferred areas of interest, as well as unmissable offers and free resources to help you successfully start your projects. *www.itgovernanceusa.com/daily-sentinel*.